RUMANIA
in pictures

Prepared by JILL McLELLAN

VISUAL GEOGRAPHY SERIES

STERLING
PUBLISHING CO., INC. NEW YORK

Oak Tree Press Co., Ltd.
London & Sydney

The Bucur Church in Bucharest was founded by Bucur the shepherd, so legend goes. It was later replaced by the present stone church whose tower roof is shaped like a shepherd's cap.

VISUAL GEOGRAPHY SERIES

Afghanistan
Alaska
Argentina
Australia
Austria
Belgium and Luxembourg
Berlin—East and West
Brazil
Bulgaria
Canada
The Caribbean (English-
  Speaking Islands)
Ceylon
Chile
Colombia
Czechoslovakia
Denmark
Ecuador
England
Ethiopia
Fiji
Finland
France
French Canada
Ghana
Greece
Guatemala
Hawaii
Holland
Honduras
Hong Kong
Hungary
Iceland
India
Indonesia
Iran
Iraq
Ireland
Islands of the
  Mediterranean
Israel

Italy
Jamaica
Japan
Kenya
Korea
Kuwait
Lebanon
Liberia
Malaysia and Singapore
Mexico
Morocco
Nepal
New Zealand
Norway
Pakistan
Panama and the Canal
  Zone
Peru
The Philippines
Poland
Portugal
Puerto Rico
Rumania
Russia
Scotland
South Africa
Spain
Surinam
Sweden
Switzerland
Tahiti and the
  French Islands of
  the Pacific
Taiwan
Tanzania
Thailand
Turkey
Venezuela
Wales
West Germany
Yugoslavia

PICTURE CREDITS

The publishers wish to thank the following for the photographs used in this book: The Rumanian State Tourist Bureau; Lufthansa German Airlines, New York.

Second Printing, 1972

Copyright © 1970 by Sterling Publishing Co., Inc.
419 Park Avenue South, New York, N.Y. 10016
British edition published by Oak Tree Press Co., Ltd., Nassau, Bahamas
Distributed in Australia by Oak Tree Press Co., Ltd.,
P.O. Box 34, Brickfield Hill, Sydney 2000, N.S.W.
Distributed in the United Kingdom and elsewhere in the British Commonwealth
by Ward Lock Ltd., 116 Baker Street, London W 1

Manufactured in the United States of America
All rights reserved
Library of Congress Catalog Card No.: 77-126859
ISBN 0-8069-1134-4   UK 7061 2260 7
1135-2

Skiing at Predeal.

CONTENTS

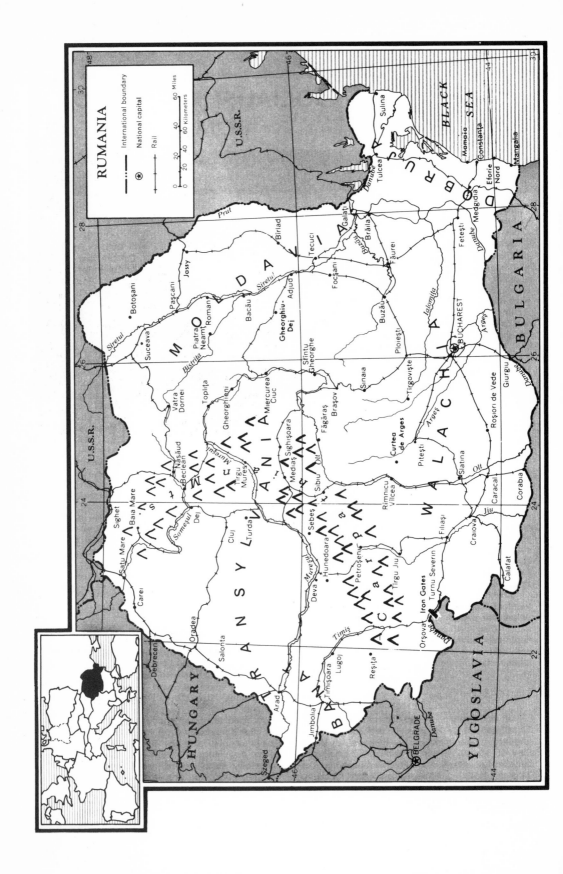

RUMANIA

International boundary
⊛ National capital
Rail

0   20   40   60 Miles
0 20 40 60 Kilometers

At Curtea de Arges (Court of Arges), near Bucharest, is the famed Episcopal Church, a 14th-century building enlarged and decorated at the beginning of the 16th century by Prince Neagoe Basarab. Its exterior is encrusted with carved stone in the Oriental style. A charming park completes the setting.

INTRODUCTION

RUMANIA IS OFTEN lumped together with Yugoslavia, Albania, Bulgaria, Greece, and European Turkey as a Balkan nation, yet the Balkan Mountain Range, for which these countries are named, bypasses Rumania completely. Instead, nature has endowed Rumania with the Carpathian Mountains, which provide visitors with beautiful scenery and a ready-made vacation area for swimming, skiing, fishing, hunting and mountain climbing. For the historically-minded, there are the old Orthodox monasteries nestled in the mountains, and the ruins of ancient Greek fishing villages along the Black Sea.

Rumania has had a turbulent and sad past, with first Turkey and then European powers overrunning its land and exploiting its natural resources. Today it is out to get the best possible trade arrangements with both Western countries and fellow countries of the Eastern European Communist bloc. To put this across, Rumania's leaders have had to speak up to Moscow, a political move which makes Westerners sympathetic to their régime.

The Government can look back on an impressive record of increased social welfare and educational opportunities for its people during

Sucevita is one of a cluster of northern Moldavian churches built in the 15th and 16th centuries by ruling princes or wealthy landowners, and known for their frescoes both outside and inside. Although the overhanging eaves have helped protect the outside frescoes from rain and snow, it is still a mystery how the dyes have survived and stayed so bright all these years.

recent years. But more important, it has led the country in a scheme of rapid industrialization and a fantastic growth rate. This has meant sacrifices on the part of the people so that one worker complains: "They're de-Balkanizing us. We're supposed to gobble our lunch in a half hour in a canteen. No more two-hour lunches dawdling over a cup of coffee." Nevertheless, it is the hard-working Rumanians with their great pride in a common Latin heritage that have helped put the miracle over.

The Olt River cuts through the southern Carpathian Mountains, with a string of spas and monasteries along its banks. Before the river flows into the Danube, the land around it flattens out. The Olt overflows its banks in the spring, and in the summer the flooded land supports a rich crop of grain.

I. THE LAND

RUMANIA, IN THE southeast corner of Europe, is a bit smaller than Great Britain, and about the size of Oregon, U.S.A. Its population of over 20,000,000 is ten times greater than Oregon's, but considerably smaller than Great Britain's 55,000,000. Rumania is at the crossroads of ancient trade routes between Asia and Europe, and even today its position is ideal for trading with both Western Europe, and the Soviet Union, with which it shares a long boundary. Through the Strait of Bosporus, on the Black Sea, Rumania's ships can reach countries bordering on the Mediterranean. Hungary lies to the west, Yugoslavia to the southwest, and Bulgaria to the south.

TOPOGRAPHY

The geography of the country varies widely—lofty mountains and broad plateaus, rolling foothills dotted with orchards, fertile plains and a sunny seacoast. Spread over this landscape are caverns, lakes and forests.

The Carpathian Mountains of Central Europe run through part of Czechoslovakia, Poland and the Soviet Union's Ukraine before ending in Rumania. As can be seen on the map, they make a semi-circle through the heart of the country.

A continuation of the Alps, the Carpathians are made up of many types of rock, and have many extinct volcanoes. In the course of time

A tourist attraction in the Carpathians is the Babele or "Old Woman" rocks. Experts argue whether the rocks have been eroded into this shape or were ancient religious sculptures.

these rocks have been broken down by wind, water and change of temperature into wild shapes, giving rise to many legends. But these mountains, for the most part, are friendly and not nearly the majestic height of the Himalayas or Andes. Their smaller size makes them more able to serve the pleasures and needs of men. Through the centuries they have been a stronghold against invading armies. Today they are the home of many independent farmers who want to keep their private property in a nation that preaches the advantages of state ownership. The highest mountain in the country, almost in its middle, is Moldoveanu, rising to a height of 8,346 feet.

Certain rock formations and depressions in the ground make it clear that glaciers once covered the Carpathians. However, many of the rocks are now concealed by forests, and clear mountain lakes have filled in the hollows carved out long ago by ice.

One characteristic of the Carpathians is the wide depressions between the mountains that have been given the name of "countries" in the past, such as the Maramures and Oas countries in the north. These countries once formed political or military states, each with separate traditions and folk arts.

There are many rivers and passes that make it easy to cross through the mountains. Among

The Bicaz Gorges, carved out by the Bicaz River, are walls of limestone rising 1,000 feet. The river and curving road find their way as best they can through the narrow canyons. Above the gorges is a new hydro-electric power dam, which has reduced the flow of the river.

This road through the Carpathians probably was first laid out during the Roman occupation, and was a busy trade route during the Middle Ages. Today it is a tourist attraction, wending its way through magnificent scenery. In the distance is Bran Castle.

the most scenic are the Bicaz River, which cuts its way through limestone cliffs, and the Predeal Pass. Most of the rivers start in the Carpathians and drain eventually into the Danube, which runs along most of the southern border. The Somesul River in the north links the country with the eastern plain of Hungary, while the Muresul River links the interior with the plains in the western part of Rumania.

Although Rumania is divided into 16 administrative districts today, the boundaries of its old provinces roughly correspond to natural regions.

TRANSYLVANIA

Encircled within the Carpathians is Transylvania, a plateau whose untouched beauty makes it a delight for visitors. Bram Stoker, author of the *Dracula* books, describes the

castle of the terrible Count Dracula in Transylvania as "on the wall of a terrible precipice. A stone falling from the window would fall a thousand feet without touching anything. As far as the eye can reach is a sea of green tree-tops, with occasionally a deep rift where there is a chasm." There are indeed castles in Transylvania (Bran and Hunedoara are two famous ones), but they are quite free of mystery compared with Dracula's.

The visitor from Rumania's capital, Bucharest, is struck by the difference evident in the towns—high-pitched red roofs and narrow twisting alleyways, and even the weather seems cooler here. Sinaia and Predeal are among the chief mountain resorts in Transylvania, and Brasov is the principal city of the region, and second largest in Rumania. In the Retezat

Hunedoara Castle existed as a fortress in the 14th century and was gradually transformed into a residence. Damaged by fire in 1854, the castle is now under restoration. It successfully combines architectural styles that have been popular in Rumania through the ages. Once a town of furriers and tanners, Hunedoara now has two open hearth furnaces that produce tons of steel each year.

Red Lake dates from 1838 when a landslide dammed the Bicaz River to create a splendid vacation spot. Today the white stumps of the forest still stick up above the surface of the lake. Rowers no doubt keep a sharp eye out for these hazards.

Brasov is Rumania's second largest city, with more than 260,000 people. Many of them work in the city's truck and tractor factories. The charming low-gabled houses of old Brasov contrast with the new buildings.

Calimanesti, on the Olt River, is a health resort with mineral springs recommended for the treatment of digestive troubles.

Busteni, with a health resort and paper mill, is nestled in the Prahova River near Sinaia. The steep mountains near the town are great for climbing.

Predeal, the highest mountain resort in Rumania, has cosy mountain chalets and an ideal winter climate for skiing.

Mountain Range is Rumania's biggest national park, with more than 80 glacial lakes.

MOLDAVIA

Between the Carpathians and the Prut River, in the northeast, lies Moldavia. The western part is mountainous, while the east, between the Siretul and Prut Rivers, is a plain or steppe, good for growing grains. Northern Moldavia is famous for its painted churches whose outside walls illustrate Biblical or historic scenes. Some of these show cruel Turks and were intended as propaganda to arouse hatred for the invader. The principal towns of Moldavia are Jassy, its former capital, and Galati, which has one of the largest steel plants in Europe.

BANAT

The southern part of the country contains rich farmland in the low land along the Danube. The southwest province of Banat, meaning

Jassy, the former capital of Moldavia, is at a crossroads of ancient trade routes. In the 1800's the city was a headquarters for the movement to unite the states that today form Rumania. Industry in Jassy includes furniture and antibiotics factories, ironworks, and textile mills. The city is proud of its many scientific and cultural institutes.

13

Ten miles from the heart of Bucharest is the Palace of Mogosoaia, built in 1703 by Prince Brancoveanu in what was later called the Brancovan style—a blending of Rumanian folk designs with Renaissance architecture. The buildings are symmetrical, with stone columns supporting graceful arches. Residents of Bucharest come to Mogosoaia to enjoy the park surrounding the palace, and swim in the lake.

frontier, is an extension of the farming plain of Hungary and northern Yugoslavia. Some of the lower Carpathian Mountains of the Banat attract skiers in the winter.

WALACHIA

In the central part of the south is the plain of Walachia. Bucharest, with a population of 1,500,000 people, is the former capital of Walachia and now capital of the entire country. North of Bucharest is Ploesti, with its famous

The narrow Dambovita River slices through Bucharest, with most of the business district on one side, and parks and lakes on the other. According to legend, the name Bucharest comes from a shepherd named Bucur who was attracted by the beauty of the Dambovita and settled in the area.

Tourists on an excursion drift among the lily pads and rich vegetation of the Danube Delta. The Danube was first mentioned by the Egyptians and the Greeks, who called the river Istros. The Romans called it Danubius at the head of the river, and Ister at the mouth. The Greek historian Polybius (201–120 B.C.) mentioned the quantities of ooze carried by the river into the Black Sea, and warned of sand banks dangerous to navigators.

oil fields, and beyond these industrial areas is rural Walachia, where farmland, vineyards and orchards lie in hollow valleys.

DOBRUJA

In the southeast is the Dobruja, where the Danube swings north, branching out into three arms of water and flowing into the Black Sea. Where the river divides the Danube Delta begins. At one time the Black Sea was lower, and the Delta was a wide plain through which the Danube flowed to the Black Sea. Then through the centuries the sea became higher

Boulevard Magheru is the heart of Bucharest's shopping district. After World War II, mansions of rich merchants along the boulevard were replaced by the modern buildings seen here.

15

Mangalia, the most modern of Rumania's seaside resorts, is built on the ruins of an ancient city founded by the Greeks in the 6th century B.C., and so there are ruins to be seen. Sheltered from the north wind by an oak forest, its location is ideal.

than it is today, and flooded the Delta. Now the water is slowly receding and the Delta is in the process of another change. The Delta's scenery is breath-taking, with all sorts of plants and animals that find nourishment in the water.

Along the Black Sea, the Dobruja is well populated with resort towns and the seaport of Constanta. Elsewhere there are fewer people since rains wash away so much of the topsoil that the land is not suitable for farming.

A lone egret stands in the waters of the Danube Delta, whose three branches flow into the Black Sea. The Delta covers more than 1,000,000 acres and is a rich natural refuge for animal life. Many flamingos, cormorants, pelicans, swans, herons and egrets nest in the Delta's shifting islands of reeds.

At Costinesti, sand pounding against the rocks through the ages has created an interesting natural sculpture.

NATURAL RESOURCES

Rumania is lucky to have large deposits of oil which have helped its industrial development. In the past these were chiefly found near Ploesti and Bacau, but new sources have been discovered in recent years near Arges and in western Walachia. Natural gas used for heating homes and as a raw material for fertilizer is often taken from the same wells that give crude oil.

The new city of Gheorghiu-Dej near Bacau has grown up since 1955 to take advantage of the

Constanta, on the Black Sea, is one of Rumania's oldest cities. It is built over the ruins of the ancient Greek colony of Tomis, founded more than 2,500 years ago. It was to Constanta that the Roman poet Ovid came in 8 A.D., driven into exile by Emperor Augustus after being involved in a scandal. Crooked streets and the Oriental look of mosques add quaintness to the modern city. For amateur archeologists there is a museum, an open-air archeological exhibit, and a Roman ruin noted for its mosaics.

oil, salt and natural gas deposits nearby. These are made into caustic soda, chlorine, insecticides, plastics and synthetic rubber.

Large deposits of copper, lead, zinc, bauxite, manganese, bismuth, mercury and silver are also found in Rumania. In addition, sources of iron ore and coal have made it possible to build great steel mills at Hunedoara, Risita and Bucharest.

CLIMATE

Although the climate of Rumania is generally like that of continental Europe, there are variations. The colder climate in the high mountains has an average summer temperature of 40 degrees, and an average winter temperature of 18 degrees. A warmer climate with a greater range is found in the basins and plateaus, with hot summers averaging 70 degrees and cold winters averaging 21 degrees. In the plains and lowlands there are hot summers averaging 73 degrees and cold winters of about 23 degrees average.

In Bucharest, the average maximum temperature in January is 33 degrees, the average minimum, 20 degrees. In July, the hottest month, the average maximum is 86 degrees, the minimum, 61 degrees. This swing between great summer heat and severe winter cold is

A fisherman pulls in his net among the tall rushes of the Danube Delta.

18

There may be snow on the ground, but these skiers at Poiana Brasov are enjoying a barbecue out of doors.

typical of the plains. Autumn is the most agreeable time of year.

Rainfall varies, the lowest being recorded on the Black Sea coast, the highest in the mountains. There are heavy rains in the spring, less in summer and autumn. Flooding of the Danube can cause great damage, as demonstrated in the spring of 1970.

PLANTS AND ANIMALS

The assortment of plants and animals is as varied as the regions of the country. The mountains are the hide-out of the bearded vulture and the chamois, a small goatlike antelope. Deer, bears, wolves, boars, lynxes, squirrels and martens (like large weasels) are also found. Trout are plentiful in the mountain steams. Fir and spruce forests cover the mountains.

In the steppes or plains, short and tall grasses grow where the land has not been cultivated. The tall grasses are high enough to conceal a man on horseback. Where civilization has not driven them out, rodents, hares, and birds such as the bustard (a heavy, long-legged game bird) are found.

The Danube Delta is a paradise for birds, especially in spring and autumn, when five major bird migrations pass over it. Nightingales, egrets, spoonbills, cormorants, geese, northern ducks, eagles and ospreys live in the Delta in different seasons. On the east bank of one channel is a reservation where the only large pelican colony of Europe nests. White willows or black poplars grow along the banks in sediment deposited by yearly floods. Floating plants such as water lilies and crowfoot lie on

The Sovata mineral springs are in a hilly region near Lake Ursu, where an Alpine climate prevails. The waters are recommended for rheumatic diseases.

19

A flock of pelicans take wing over the Delta marshes.

Is this lynx napping or waiting to pounce on his prey?

More than 60 species of fresh water fish, including the caviar-producing sturgeon, pike, carp and trout are caught in the Danube. Here, fishermen in small skiffs are towed by a motor boat.

The century-old Cismigiu Garden in Bucharest includes lakes and a small zoo with pelicans and other creatures.

The Carpathian red stag is a rare animal protected by conservation laws.

the surface of the pools. Reeds in the Delta are harvested in November, when birds have gone to their winter homes. Cellulose from the reeds is used in making fabrics and tires.

Lumbering out of the forest is a brown bear, some of which weigh as much as 700 pounds. Bears attack cattle or sheep brought up to graze on the Rumanian mountain ranges during the summer, and are a threat to shepherds.

In Adamclisi, 40 miles from Constanta, stand the ruins of a monument by Roman Emperor Trajan to celebrate his victory over the people of Scythia Minor, the present day Dobruja. In front is a model of what the monument might have looked like.

2. HISTORY

ABOUT 5,000 YEARS before Christ a culture existed in what is now Rumania that was remarkably advanced for its time. Archeologists have uncovered sites in Moldavia and Transylvania dating from 4200 B.C., but more recent diggings in Moldavia have turned up bits of pottery even older. It is not clear who these early people were.

About 2000 B.C., Indo-European tribes, the Thracians from the west, drifted into the region, ranging over large areas from the Aegean and Adriatic Seas to the western shores of Asian Turkey. One group of these tribes, the Dacians, lived in the region that is now Rumania. They established contact with several slave-owning Greek colonies along the Black Sea—Histria, Callatis and Tomis. The kings of Dacia protected these cities for centuries.

The Greek historian Herodotus described the Thracians as farmers who herded cattle, grew grain and vines, and kept bees. But the Dacians were the most brave, he wrote.

By the 3rd century B.C. the Dacians were organized into a strong state with a high level of civilization. In the 1st century B.C., a great king, Burbista, ruled an empire that stretched across a large section of southeast Europe and managed to defend his kingdom against Julius

Caesar. But by 106 A.D. Dacia was conquered by the Romans, led by Trajan, and was to remain a province of the Roman Empire until 271.

The Black Sea cities were linked to the rest of the Roman Empire by the Danube and by a road which entered Dacia to the west by way of the Iron Gates, where the Danube breaks through the mountains near Turnu Severin. This was the great marching route of the Roman legions, and it also connected the chief cities of Dacia, in which the Romans built villas, forts, baths and monuments celebrating their victories.

Trajan found gold and copper in Dacia, and many Dacian men were taken prisoner to be sold in slave markets. Dacia was also valuable for its fertile land. Dacia benefitted from Roman rule, which brought a time of prosperity and calm, and many soldiers and citizens from all over the civilized world came to settle there. It is interesting to note that even though Dacia was one of the last lands taken by the Romans, and only under their rule for a century and a half, the Romans made more of an impact there than in other Eastern European countries which they occupied. The basis of the Rumanian language is from the Latin, and even the name of the country is derived from that of the Romans. Perhaps this impact was because of the heavy settlement of the country by Roman colonists.

From the 3rd century on, the Romans could no longer defend Dacia against the barbarian tribes that were overrunning Europe. Avars, Goths, Slavs and Bulgars swept across what is now Rumania. Surviving in the mountains were the Latin-speaking peasants who had stayed on after the Roman withdrawal. Even today there are pockets of people (Vlachs) in Bulgaria and Yugoslavia speaking dialects of Rumanian. Under the Bulgars, a return to government took form, and when Bulgaria's King Boris was converted to Christianity, he brought this

Hercules, the Greek deity for whom Herculane was named, stands in the middle of the resort buildings.

Sighisoara, where the Saxons settled in the early Middle Ages, still looks like a medieval town, with its fortress and monastery. The clock tower, at the entrance to the fortress, has seven figures that appear one by one on each of the days of the week. Others of the nine towers have names such as the Ropers' Tower, Butchers' Tower and Furriers' Tower, named for trades of the Middle Ages. The modern city grew up beside the fortress, and blends well with it.

religion to the Vlachs as well as to his own country.

About the 10th century, Transylvania was taken over by the Magyars, or Hungarians, a group of tribes originally from Central Asia. Then under Hungarian leadership, Germans, called Saxons, began to establish a number of fortified cities such as Cluj, Sibiu, and Sighisoara, in Transylvania. These were not the same Saxons who had invaded and settled England 500 years earlier, but Germans from the Rhineland. Hungarian princes came in as administrators and governed Transylvania under a form of feudalism. The feudal states, or voivodates, were ruled by the *voivodes*, or princes. The peasants were slaves to their prince for a plot of land, and often lost their lives in the continual warfare between states.

With the coming of the Hungarians, some Rumanians, or Vlachs, were driven south out of the Carpathians. One group settled in the area later forming Walachia, which gets its name from the Vlachs. The other went into what was to become Moldavia. The Vlachs mingled with Slavs and Tatars already in these areas. Not until 1859 were Moldavia and Walachia to become united as Rumania.

In the early Middle Ages, Saxons settled in Sibiu, in Transylvania, which even today has a well-preserved medieval section. In the 15th century the town surrounded itself with new walls thick enough to keep out the invading Turks. Today the Germanic influence survives in the neat tiled houses, Lutheran faith, and old Saxon dialect. The most interesting spot for visitors is the Brukenthal Museum, named after an 18th-century governor of Transylvania, whose collection of historic and art objects is displayed in his former house.

Vlad the Impaler ruled Walachia from 1456–1462. The name "Impaler" apparently came from his torturing subjects who committed crimes. After cracking down on lawbreakers, legend says that robberies were reduced and he brought in a more lawful society.

WALACHIA

Walachia was first set up as a state under the thumb of Transylvania in the 13th century. But one of its princes, Basarab, defeated the Hungarian King Charles I Robert in 1330 and gained independence for the new state. In the early days, the Hungarians were the enemies, but during the reign of Mircea the Old (1386–1418) the Turks became the main aggressors. The Turkish, or Ottoman, Empire was gradually taking over countries to the south— Serbia (now part of Yugoslavia), Bulgaria, and the Byzantine or Eastern Roman Empire. The Ottomans made Constantinople, capital of the Byzantine Empire, their capital. Today Constantinople is Istanbul.

Walachia got help from Transylvania in fighting the Turks, but the two were defeated in 1396. Although Mircea later returned to the throne, Walachia was forced to yield to Turkey. In taking over countries in the early years, the Turks at first would let the local prince or ruler remain, asking only that he pay tribute (money or goods) to Turkey. Countries often kept their Christian religion, and their boundaries were undisturbed. In short, life was not too bad under the conquerors, since they were good administrators and kept the various princes from fighting among themselves. However, as time went on, the Ottomans became increasingly harsh on Christians. Christian children were taken from their parents to serve in the administration of the Ottoman Empire. Janis-

Peasant fortresses, like this one at Homorod in Transylvania, were built around a church and used as a defense against Turk and Tatar invasions.

Forbidding Bran Castle was built by merchants in the 14th century and German knights lived there for a long time. Never conquered by the Turks, Bran served as a toll station between Transylvania and Walachia and is now a museum.

saries, the Turkish professional soldiers, were stationed in the Balkans and were notorious for cruelties inflicted on the enslaved populations.

For a time the balance of power shifted in Walachia and the Hungarians, under Janos Hunyadi, defeated the weak Walachian princes. They put Vlad the Impaler on the throne, and this strict prince was able to defy the Turks for a while. But with his death resistance crumbled, and one prince after another was a tool of the Turks.

MOLDAVIA

The state of Moldavia was founded slightly after Walachia, taking shape in 1359 under Bogdan I. One of the early princes was Petru Musat, a relative of the Basarab family of Walachia. He held the state in the interest of his leader, Mircea the Old. Petru married the sister of the King of Poland, forming a tie with that nation—ever after there would be shifting alliances with Poland. At times Moldavia would

turn to Poland for help against the Turks, and then when stronger Poland would dominate, the two states would fight one another. A similar pattern of on-and-off friendship existed between Hungary and Walachia.

Stefan the Great, an able organizer, clever diplomat and great commander, was to prove a leading defender of Christianity against the Turks. But more important, he built a ring of forts to defend his principality. One historian has said that the Turks in Moldavia fought against walls of granite. Behind these defenses, churches and palaces sprang up. Suceava, the early capital of Moldavia, flourished under Stefan, with trade links to all corners of Europe and the Near East. Progress was made cul-

turally, as Stefan encouraged the development of handicrafts in the towns, and the Moldavian school of architecture was begun under his reign. This golden age came to a close when Stefan's son Petru Rares was defeated by the Turks in 1538.

MICHAEL THE BRAVE

The Hungarians, who had held Transylvania for 400 years, suffered a crushing defeat from the Turks at the battle of Mohacs in 1526. By the middle of the 1500's, the Turks had a strong foothold throughout Moldavia, Walachia and Transylvania. But they reckoned without Michael the Brave, Prince of Walachia, who came to the throne in 1593. He obtained a loan

Near Putna Monastery, in the northwest, is the cave of Daniel the Hermit, counselor to Stefan the Great. Stefan founded Putna, and no doubt stayed at the monastery when he came to consult with Daniel.

Michael the Brave, ruler of Walachia from 1593 to 1601, won brilliant victories against the Turks and Tatars. To gain further strength against the aggressors, he conquered Transylvania and Moldavia, bringing the three states for the first time under one rule.

of 400,000 ducats, paid off the Turkish ruler, and took the throne from Alexander, the reigning prince. Then he brashly massacred Turkish guards, and with the Prince of Moldavia invaded the lands south of the Danube. He won brilliant victories against the Turks, and defeated the armies of the prince of Transylvania, Andrei Bathory. Michael proclaimed himself ruler of Moldavia, Transylvania and Walachia. He is a great folk hero in Rumania today, since the Vlachs of all three states were united for the first time.

The union of the three states was short-lived, since Hungary moved back into Transylvania and drove Michael's army out. Poland invaded Moldavia and put a friendly prince back on the throne, only to have the Turks take over again in 1618. Turkey took over Walachia and put a puppet prince on the throne.

In the early 1600's the capital of Walachia was moved from Tirgoviste to Bucharest, at a safe distance from Hungarian Transylvania, from which attacks were a constant threat. Turkey began taking a bigger part in choosing the princes of Walachia and Moldavia. The Turkish choices were often of Greek origin. The first important Greek prince was Serban Cantacuzino, Prince of Walachia, who helped the Turks in their unsuccessful penetration of Hapsburg's Austrian Empire. Defeated at the gates of Vienna in 1683, the Turks began to lose their possessions in Europe. At the height of their power the Turks had penetrated as far as Hungary, and held all the land of present-day Rumania.

In 1688, when Serban died, printing presses turned out the first Rumanian Bibles. Cultural changes were continued under the rule of his nephew, Constantin Brancoveanu, who introduced a new architectural style. For a while Brancoveanu was able to keep friendly with the Polish King, Turkish Sultan, Hapsburg Emperor and Russian Tsar. But his mistake was in asking Peter the Great of Russia for help against Turkey, for which he was executed by the Turks at Constantinople.

RULE OF THE PHANARIOTS

At the beginning of the 1700's, Turkey felt new threats from Russia and Austria as Moldavian and Walachian princes tried to join forces with those two powers. To exert more control, the Turks sold the principalities to wealthy Greek merchants from the Phanar section of Constantinople. These princes, who became known as the Phanariots, established a cruel régime, since they tried to get everything out of the states that they could in a short time. Peasants were forced to work for their masters, and pay taxes to the sultan, prince and boyars (native noblemen) as well.

Several Russian-Turkish wars took place in

the late 1700's with Walachia and Moldavia as the battleground. In 1791, when it looked as though Turkey was winning and would inflict new cruelties, a group of boyars asked Austria and Russia for a new effort to end Phanariot rule. Though this appeal was unsuccessful, it was an early gesture of Rumanian solidarity against foreigners.

The dream of independence for the Rumanian states was to become a reality in the next century, but not before more blood was shed. After a new Russian-Turkish outbreak, Russia lost out on its wish to add Moldavia and Walachia to its empire, but was given Bessarabia, at the tip of southeast Moldavia, under the terms of the Peace of Bucharest in 1812.

In 1821, Tudor Vladimirescu led a rebellion against the Phanariots which failed. But Turkey agreed thereafter to have local rather than Greek rulers.

In 1828 the Russians again invaded Moldavia and Walachia, occupying them until 1834. Under the Russian General Paul Kisseleff, new constitutions were written for the states, which placed law-making power in an elected body. But the constitutions benefitted the boyars and not the peasants, so the stage was set for revolutions in 1848, in which the peasants fought for their rights.

CREATION OF RUMANIA

At the Congress of Paris in 1856, Moldavia and Walachia were made independent principalities within the Ottoman Empire. Soon after they were united under Alexander Cuza, and used the name of Rumania for the first time, but still within the Ottoman Empire. Cuza brought in a series of land reforms, angering the boyars and clergy by making them break up

their lands. He could not please the peasants either, who felt the reforms did not go far enough. So Carol of Hohenzollern, a German prince, took the throne in 1866 and served until 1914.

Not that all was calm under his rule. In 1878, Rumania fought with Russia against Turkey and finally shed itself completely of Turkish domination. After the war Russia gained southern Bessarabia, which it had handed back to Rumania in 1859. In return, Rumania won the northern Dobruja, giving the country one of the Danube's mouths as an outlet on the Black Sea. Carol's reign did see the development of a parliamentary government, although it did not really represent the people. The Liberals aimed to build a strong middle class and were pro-French. The Conservatives, composed mainly of the old boyar class, leaned toward Russia. The Young Conservatives, on the other hand, sought ties with Germany, since they had largely been educated there. These factions were each trying to dominate the government.

29

Peles Castle, in Sinaia, is a former royal summer residence built between 1875 and 1883 for King Carol I, and is now open to the public. Built of stone, timber, brick and marble, its architecture is German Renaissance, with bits of French Rococo and Moorish thrown in.

Rumanian soldiers step over fallen comrades in the painting, "The Attack of Smirdan" by Nicolae Grigoresco. It depicts a scene from the War of Independence, 1877–1878.

THE BALKAN WARS

The outbreak of the First Balkan War in 1912 marked the next foreign crisis, pitting Turkey against Bulgaria, Greece, Serbia and Montenegro. (The latter two are republics of Yugoslavia today.) Rumania tried to stay out of it.

But when Bulgaria attacked its allies in 1913, some 500,000 Rumanian soldiers moved in and occupied the southern Dobruja. In this Second Balkan War, Bulgaria was roundly defeated and lost some land to Turkey that it had gained in the First Balkan War.

WORLD WAR I

When King Carol died in 1914 his son, Ferdinand, took power, marrying Princess Marie of Edinburgh, a granddaughter of England's Queen Victoria. When World War I broke out, Rumania again tried to stay neutral. However, it was only a question of time before the country got involved on the side of England and France. At the peace table, Rumania gained Transylvania and Banat, which had been held

by Austria-Hungary. Bessarabia was taken from Russia, which had been defeated by Germany and was in a state of civil war.

After the war the government was unstable, with laws being changed to suit the party currently in power. The peasants, however, demanded and got a new constitution with more land reforms.

CAROL II

The death of King Ferdinand in 1927 created a crisis in the monarchy. His 5-year-old grandson Michael I became king, since his father Carol II had given up rights to the throne in 1925. But Carol renewed his claim and finally took over in 1930.

Adding to this unrest was the world economic crisis, reflected in strikes by railroad and oil

The Monument to Heroes of the Air in Bucharest commemorates Rumanian pilots who lost their lives in World War I.

31

Bucharest's Arch of Triumph was built in the 1930's along the lines of the more famous Paris arch. In the distance is the government printing house, where editorial offices of the main newspapers and magazines and the Rumanian Press Agency are located. The printing house was built after World War II in a heavy style nicknamed "Stalin Gothic," of which one finds examples in Warsaw and Moscow. Presses at the printing house turn out some 2,000,000 copies of newspapers and magazines each day.

workers in Rumania. Many in desperation turned to the new Communist or Fascist parties.

The government of the 1930's was dominated by the terrorist tactics of the Fascist, anti-Semitic Iron Guard, whose members wanted to align the country with Germany and Italy. Most Communist leaders were jailed, but a government exchange of political prisoners with Moscow sent Communists of Rumania's minority races to Russia. Those of "pure" Rumanian ethnic background, largely from the trade unions, were jailed until 1944, among them Gheorghe Gheorghiu-Dej.

WORLD WAR II

The Iron Guard took Rumania into World War II on the side of Germany. In June, 1940, the Germans insisted that Bessarabia be returned to Russia and two months later the Germans made Rumania return northern Transylvania to Hungary. After the German attack on Russia, Rumania suffered severe defeats from 1943 on, with people at home starving.

King Michael who had succeeded his father Carol, after Carol's death in exile, led a coup and

booted out the Iron Guard dictatorship, on August 23, 1944. He signed an armistice with the Allies and confirmed the return of Bessarabia to Russia, gaining back northern Transylvania.

THE PEOPLE'S REPUBLIC

An Allied Control Council, with a Russian as chairman, was sent to Rumania to help run the country until the Peace Treaty was signed in February, 1947. With the added factor of the Russian Army in the country, it was natural that the Communists won elections and took over easily. In December, 1947, King Michael stepped down and the Communists proclaimed Rumania a People's Republic. A constitution like Russia's was adopted in 1948.

RUMANIA TODAY

By 1952 the government had replaced Communists whose loyalties were to Rumania with pro-Soviet Communists. Gheorghe Gheorghiu-Dej became premier in 1952 and a new constitution was put in effect emphasizing Rumania's independence of the Soviet Union.

Since late 1961, Rumanian Communism has become less dependent on Moscow. Along with this has come a more moderate Communism without Stalinist pressure. Nearly all political prisoners were released in the 1960's, and the government has tried to strengthen its position in the country by attracting different groups such as the intellectuals and farmers who were previously against Communism. Party membership has grown.

In front of the Military Academy in Bucharest is a monument to the nation's heroes.

Leadership since the late 1950's has been stable. When Gheorghiu-Dej died in 1965, Nicolae Ceausescu gradually assumed power, starting as party chief and becoming chief of state in December, 1967.

The real test of independence came in August, 1968, when the Soviet Union entered Czechoslovakia with all its Communist allies, except Rumania. The Russians feared unsettled political conditions in Czechoslovakia could spread to other European Communist powers. Would Rumania be invaded next? Rumanian crowds gathered around the Communist Party headquarters in Bucharest listening to the news on transistor radios. Their sympathy was behind Ceausescu in his attack on the Soviet Union and promise of help to the Czechs.

Rumania's independent line of action appeared to have been accepted by the Russians, for no retaliation took place.

The Palace of the Republic (older building in the middle), built in 1930 and used until 1937 as a royal palace, now houses several museums. The National Gallery section has works by Rumanian artists such as Nicolae Grigoresco, as well as icons, manuscripts, carved furniture and sculpture. In the Gallery of World Art are works by European artists. Attached to the Palace is Congress Hall (middle foreground).

3. GOVERNMENT

As IN OTHER Communist countries, the Rumanian Communist Party is the real machine that runs the government, and regulates every aspect of Rumanian life. This is spelled out in the 1952 constitution, patterned after the Soviet one. It says that the party is the "leading force of the organizations of the working people as well as of the state organs and institutions."

THE SOCIALIST REPUBLIC

The radical wing of the Socialists, and the trade unions, formed the basis of a Communist Party in 1921. But arguing among different factions and repression by the government in power kept it small. Not until December, 1947, was the Rumanian People's Republic declared.

A new constitution adopted in 1965 changed the name of the country from the Rumanian People's Republic to the Socialist Republic of Rumania. A socialist republic is considered to be further advanced on the road to Communism than a people's republic.

When Nicolae Ceausescu came into full power in 1967 he eliminated about 10,000 government positions in the interest of efficiency, but it was actually to strengthen his position. The security police was placed under tighter control. At the same time, additional rights were given prisoners, and Ceausescu tried to create a more relaxed climate overall.

The Communist government of Rumania, as it operates within the country, could be called moderate. The average Rumanian seldom questions his leaders, as he might do in Hungary or Yugoslavia. Yet he probably has more freedom than under Bulgaria's or Czechoslovakia's régimes.

LEGISLATURE

The Grand National Assembly, with 465 deputies from different districts, is the legislature or parliament of the country. It meets twice yearly for a few days and does little legislative work. Important laws and the budget are discussed by the Assembly and usually adopted unanimously. It also appoints members to the State Council, Council of Ministers and the Supreme Court.

STATE COUNCIL

The State Council's 20 odd members carry on the Assembly's business when it is not in session. It has the power to issue decrees with the force of law.

COUNCIL OF MINISTERS

The Council of Ministers consists of a president, several vice presidents and a varying number of ministers, as well as the chairmen of certain commissions such as those for planning and grain collection. Responsible to the State Council and the Assembly, the Council of Ministers nevertheless has wide powers to carry out the state economic plan, assure public order, defend the interests of the state, protect the rights of citizens, etc. It executes policies of the Communist Party, and has the authority to issue decisions and orders.

JUDICIARY

The Supreme Court is the highest court of the country. Its members, serving five year terms, control the activities of the 18 regional courts and local people's courts.

LOCAL GOVERNMENT

Units of local government range from the region, which is the highest administrative division, to the village, the smallest. One of the 16 regions, populated mostly by Hungarians, has special self-governing rights. At each level the governing bodies or people's councils carry out the laws of the central government and decide certain local matters.

PARTY ORGANIZATION

Parallel to the different levels of the government are different branches of the Communist Party which write many of the directives carried out by the state. At the lowest level are the Party Congresses (held infrequently). Delegates

United States President Richard Nixon and his wife visited Rumania in the summer of 1969, and crowds greeted them with "Traiasca prietenia noastra!" (Long live our friendship!) Critics of the visit pointed out that Rumanian office workers had been let out for the day to swell the crowd watching the motorcade, but it was still important that an American President was visiting a Communist nation for the first time in 25 years. With the Nixons in the photo are Rumanian President Nicolae Ceausescu and his wife.

elect a Central Committee which in turn elects the policy-making Praesidium and the largely administrative Secretariat. In the past, government members have held corresponding, but separate, positions in the party. But under Ceausescu even the illusion of separate state and party authority has been done away with, and many state and party jobs have been merged. This leaves no doubt that the party runs the government.

ELECTIONS

Election for the Grand National Assembly deputies as well as municipal, borough, village and communal people's councils are held every four years. In the elections of March, 1969, about 13,000,000 citizens 18 years and over were eligible to vote, and 99 per cent took part. They used a ballot with a single slate. Only endorsed members of the Socialist United Front (made up of the Party, trade unions, women's organizations, youth and professional people) were on the ballot. Although allowed, write-ins numbered only about 13,000, which could be taken as a strong endorsement of the government in power. There is no reason to believe there was a lack of write-ins because of fear of

harassment, especially since the constitution guarantees voting by secret ballot.

FOREIGN RELATIONS

In dealing with other countries, Rumania has had great success in steering a course independent from Russia. Although a member of the Warsaw Pact along with East Germany, Poland, Czechoslovakia, Hungary, Bulgaria and Russia, Rumania has shown skill at staying friendly with both East and West, even defying Moscow at times. Perhaps one reason it is allowed such freedom internationally is that Rumanian leaders have thus far run a stable government along orthodox Communist lines.

In the early 1950's Gheorghe Gheorghiu-Dej ousted the faction blindly devoted to Moscow, but kept calling himself a loyal Stalinist. In 1958, two years after the Hungarian revolution, which never spread to Rumania, Gheorghiu-Dej persuaded the Russians to take their soldiers home, and they went quietly.

Rumania has said it wants to develop its economy independently and not to coordinate it with the Council for Mutual Economic Assistance, an overall economic planning group of East European nations.

The biggest split with Moscow has, of course, developed over Rumania's neutrality in the Russia-China dispute. Rumania blames the arguments between the two on "differences which exist in the levels of economic and social development of these countries." Experts say Rumania has not tried to play one power off against the other, but really desires to be a peacemaker.

Another point of disagreement between Rumania and Russia is the staging of Warsaw Pact war games on Rumanian soil. Rumania has been reluctant to have its land used for such activities. In the United Nations Rumania favors Russia's policy in helping North Vietnam, but avoids taking sides.

Rumania is eager to trade with all West European powers, and exchanged ambassadors with West Germany in 1967. When Willy Brandt of West Germany suggested talks with the East European community to normalize relations, Rumania led in urging such talks.

Rumania's prime minister and foreign minister visited the United Kingdom in 1969, the first visit since World War II. Officials discussed trade agreements, disarmament and a security conference of all European countries, a proposal Rumania has long tried to promote.

In 1967, Rumania signed a three-year trade pact with Israel, and would not join in condemning Israel as the aggressor in the 1967 war with Egypt. In 1969, it became the only East European country to have full diplomatic relations with Israel. The Arabs then withdrew their ambassadors, but there is a move to win them back.

Rumania wants trade with as many nations as possible, and has even extended its influence to South America. In one year alone it signed a treaty to buy crude oil from Venezuela, worked out a plan to extract non-ferrous metals from Chilean mines, and answered a request from Bolivia for help in running properties taken from the Gulf Oil Company.

Relations with the United States have steadily improved since the mid-1960's when Voice of America broadcasts were no longer jammed, and legations in both countries were elevated to embassies.

In 1967, Rumanian Prime Minister Ion Maurer visited President Johnson in the United States. This was followed by a successful visit of President Nixon to Bucharest in 1969, the first time an American president had visited an East European Communist nation in 25 years. He and Ceausescu discussed the possibility of opening a United States-to-Rumania civil air link.

Eventually Rumania would like to become a spokesman for all neutralist nations of the world, perhaps replacing Tito of Yugoslavia. At Soviet-United States disarmament conferences it has criticized both nations for maintaining bases in foreign countries and holding war games on foreign territory. Rumania has urged a freeze on all military budgets, and has cut its own military spending.

There is no doubt that its status as a neutral nation was helped when Corneliu Manescu served as president of the United Nations General Assembly in 1967-8. This was the first time a Communist official ever held the post.

In spite of wanting to play a modest rôle in world politics, leaders are most concerned with keeping day-to-day relations with Moscow on an even keel.

Symbol of Rumania, the Atheneum in Bucharest is a concert hall and headquarters of the George Enesco State Philharmonic Orchestra. The snowy white outside of the building resembles a Greek temple with a heavy Baroque dome.

4. THE PEOPLE

OF THE 20,300,000 PEOPLE living in Rumania, 87 per cent are ethnic Rumanians. Of the minority groups remaining, 8 per cent are Hungarians, 2 per cent are Germans, and the rest are Jews, Ukrainians, Greeks, Turks and gypsies.

Those of Rumanian stock proudly trace their ancestors back to the Romans, reliving battles fought 20 centuries ago between the Dacians and Romans. They prefer the spelling "Romania" to "Rumania" or the compromise "Roumania," which both point up the Western influence. The Rumanian's link with a Latin past is evident in his dark eyes and features which make him look almost Italian.

The Hungarians live in Transylvania, numbering three-fourths of the local population in some towns. They are a politically significant group and are given some self-government.

Jews first came to Rumania in the late 15th century. Other Jews from Poland and Russia came during the 19th century, introducing some modern financial institutions. Many Jews have emigrated to Israel in recent years.

The gypsies, found in all Eastern Europe, make up a particularly interesting group.

Fishing canoes are beached next to a little village on the Danube River.

Horse-drawn gypsy caravans still rumble through the mountain passes of Transylvania. Even in Bucharest, one finds them living on the sidewalks not far from the big hotels, in family groups with the mother fondling the children.

The gypsies are wanderers, making their living as horse traders, basket makers or carnival people. As musicians they are in great demand in cafés and restaurants. The Romany tongue spoken by the gypsies has nothing to do with the name "Rumania," since the Romany word "rom" means simply "man."

LANGUAGE

Rumanian is a Romance language similar to Latin, but with many Slavic, German and Greek words. Rumanian was long written in the Cyrillic alphabet used in the Slavic languages. Then, in the 1800's a move developed in Transylvania to use the Latin alphabet instead, emphasizing the Roman origins of the nation. It is written with this alphabet today.

German or Hungarian is spoken by small pockets of people in Transylvania. French is heard frequently in the cities, going back to a period of close business and political ties with France before World War II.

A former royal summer residence in Bucharest, this building is now used by the Pioneers, a group of young people similar to the Scouts and Guides of Western countries. They come here after school to work on hobbies, practice musical instruments, or engage in sports.

39

A new colony of small summer cottages flanks a tent community, on the Black Sea coast.

LIVING CONDITIONS

Most Rumanians would say that life under Communism is better than under any previous government. Food is available, but lines are long in food shops and it can take two hours a day to collect an ordinary family's food needs. The biggest complaint is the shortage of clothes, appliances and cars. Moreover, quality is sometimes poor since the better goods are sold abroad. Rumanians realize that in a developing country, industrialization is more important than providing consumer goods, but they still resent having to go without certain things.

Sprawling new apartments are found on the outskirts of cities, grouped around parks. They are frequently more attractive than similar projects in other countries. Most families make out with one bedroom—two bedrooms are a luxury.

Factory workers work $8\frac{1}{2}$ hours a day, Monday through Friday with a short day on Saturday. Wages are low by Western standards, but there is often more than one wage earner in

The high-pitched thatch roofs on these homes in the Bucharest Village Museum are typical of the Bukovina region, near the Russian border. Their steep pitch helps rain water to drain off.

The Olanesti Health Resort in the valley of the Olanesti River is sheltered from cold winds by the surrounding hills. The resort has 30 springs containing various minerals.

a family, and an apartment can be had for a very low rental. Farmers on a collective farm have their houses provided, and earn a tiny monthly sum, depending on how profitable their farm is. They work longer hours than a factory worker. A lumber-jack or other manual worker may earn more than a surgeon working the same hours. This is justified by the much shorter period in which a manual worker can do productive work.

Vacations are generous, with most workers starting with paid vacations of 15 work days. Practically no one may travel outside the country, the official reason being that Rumania cannot afford the exchange of its currency into foreign money. But there are many Rumanian Black Sea resorts or mountain hotels where vacations cost next to nothing.

As in other Communist countries, emphasis is placed on health care, and government statistics show that the number of hospital beds rose 4.5

times between 1938 and 1960s. Medical care is free or available for a very low charge.

Life in the cities is pleasant, and uncrowded by Western standards. The city dweller enjoys taking a walk along the broad tree-lined boulevards and stopping to chat with friends. For entertainment, there are the cinema, ballet, opera and museums. Transportation to work is by tram, trolleybus or bicycle.

About 60 per cent of the people still live in the country, although this figure gets smaller every year. Here, families live in three-room wooden houses. Visitors enter into the middle room, or kitchen, heated by a big earthenware wood-burning stove. On one side is the family

Many rural Rumanian homes have been moved piece by piece from different sections of the country to make up the charming Village Museum in Bucharest. The houses in this restoration are furnished with authentic utensils, furniture, carpets and decorations—many have looms in them. Besides the houses, visitors can wander through little country churches and see reconstructed windmills. There is even a gold sluice, where gold mined in the mountains was once processed.

Ana Aslan is director of the Geriatrics Institute in Bucharest, whose treatments to slow the advance of old age draw people from around the world. Patients get injections of Gerovital H-3, a medicine thought to slow the aging process.

bedroom, and on the other the food storeroom. Adjoining the storeroom is the barn. At one time all farm buildings were attached to the house, since taxation was on the basis of the number of buildings. A well in the courtyard provides water.

Most farmers have organized themselves into collectives, but shepherds who spend part of the year in hilly regions have fought the trend to collectivize their lands. The state has left them alone, since collective farms work best in flat country where modern farm machinery can work efficiently and rapidly.

In the summer the shepherd lives in the mountains with his family. During the day he has only a staff and dog to ward off the bears as

The new hospital at Bacau reflects the importance placed on the health of the people. Rumania has a high ratio of doctors to population, a high life expectancy, and much of its health care is free.

Recently formed, this chorus tours Europe singing madrigals from the Elizabethan era. Here, they stand together in the Bucharest Atheneum, noted for its beautiful interior.

he watches his sheep. At night he beds his flock in an enclosure with other flocks. Each fall he returns to the valley with his family, his sheep heavy with wool and carts loaded with goat cheese.

This picture of rural Rumania is changing as the standard of village life is raised. Many villages are now electrified, and TV antennas sprout on the roofs of peasant homes. To carry out the country's educational plan, all teachers must teach several years in small towns.

Congress Hall was built in modern style in 1959 to present plays and concerts. Benny Goodman played in Congress Hall early in 1970 while on tour and had a warm reception, the Rumanian press praising his band's "passionate renditions."

Women in Bucharest stock up on groceries in this modern store. Fresh meat and vegetables are more often sold in separate shops.

FOOD

The Rumanians have an interesting style of cooking—rich, but with subtle seasonings. Some dishes have been borrowed from the Slavic, Hungarian and Turkish cultures.

Breakfast is on the light side and may include rolls, butter and jam, along with tea, milk or coffee. Boiled eggs, ham, cheese or sausage are available for a more hearty meal.

Dinner, served about 2 P.M., is the principal meal and is accompanied by wines, or *tuica*, the Rumanian plum brandy. The first course of soup has a base of meat, vegetables or noodles. It may be a *borshch* like its Russian cousin, but with more vegetables, or it may be *ciorba de perisoare*, meatball soup.

Next is the main course—quite likely garnished veal with boiled, fried or mashed potatoes. Other specialities are boiled beef, and broiled or spit-roasted chicken. A national dish, and real staple of the farmer, is *mamaliga*, a boiled cornmeal served either as a bread substitute, with stuffed cabbage or vine leaves (*sarmale*), or with poached eggs. Hot or cold,

mamaliga is delicious in melted butter or yoghurt, garnished with salted herring and cottage cheese.

All the above are accompanied by salads and vegetables such as eggplant, sharp peppers, or gherkins.

Two fishermen in the Danube Delta cook up a fish stew for supper.

44

The entrance to the famous Beer Cart Restaurant in Bucharest, right, is adorned with lamps in the form of beer kegs. This café was built in 1879 in the neo-Gothic style and is a popular meeting place of writers and artists. Lively night life in Bucharest has earned it the title "Paris of the East." Many night clubs have gypsy orchestras, dancing, jazz bands and variety shows.

For dessert there are several popular dishes: *placinte,* turnovers with various fillings; *baclava,* a Turkish cake in syrup; delicious ice cream or the pâtisserie typical of Transylvania. Fresh watermelon, cherries, apples, grapes or peaches may be served as well. Turkish coffee completes the meal.

Rumania is rich in game and fish of all kinds. In the mountains, brook trout and venison are popular, while Danube Delta cooks roast carp on spits, and make a delicious fish soup. Supper, with a basic course of grilled beef, pork or chicken, is served about 8 P.M., again with wines and brandy. The highly seasoned grilled meat balls—*mititei*—are famous at home and abroad.

ART

Rumanians are an artistic people whose creativity has found expression in every century, even when under the thumb of a foreign ruler. One example of their early art is the black pottery created by the ancient Dacians and reproduced today. It is decorated in a luminous gray, or a range of shades from gray to black.

In the 14th century, Walachia began to develop a culture inspired by Byzantine styles. This was evident in the solemn and splendid court costumes, stone monuments, and monasteries such as the one at Curtea de Arges. In Moldavia, the Byzantine influence was added to local elements to produce the monasteries at Voronet, Sucevita and a number of other locations. Besides the interesting architecture of the monastery churches, the paintings on the

Polovraci, west of Brasov, was built in the 17th century, and has a church containing lovely frescoes. Shown here are living quarters of the monks who still run the monastery.

The Stavropoleos Church, with its delicate exterior of carved stone, was built in the 1720's in a style known as Brancoveanu, and was restored in the early 1900's—an easy job since it is a sturdy structure. Any building built before 1847 and still standing is probably made of stone or brick, since that was the year the Turks burned Bucharest and all wooden buildings went up in smoke.

The Voronet Monastery Church, begun in 1488 by Stefan the Great, is set in meadows encircled by mountains and pine woods. This church is famed for the blue tones in its outdoor frescoes. The west front fresco includes a grim depiction of the Last Judgment where the River of Fire devours sinners, and angels run their spears through black devils.

churches' exteriors show a liveliness that goes beyond the Byzantine. Soon the spirit of the Italian Renaissance, coming by way of what is today Yugoslavia, contributed to more freely painted church figures in both Moldavia and Walachia.

MODERN ART

Non-religious art began in the first half of the 19th century, brought back by so.1s of the wealthy landowners who studied at art schools

The Maramures region in the northwest part of Transylvania is noted for wooden churches such as this one. Many are built entirely of wood, even down to the nails, and are a tribute to the skill of Rumanian craftsmen. Steeples, high in proportion to the rest of the building, add to their quaintness.

A celebration is in progress within the historic walls of Sucevita Monastery.

in Rome and Paris. Two such artists who were products of the Barbizon School in Paris were Nicolae Grigorescu and Ion Andreescu. Grigorescu painted many landscapes showing peasant life united with nature. Andreescu showed a sadder side of peasant life. In the early 1900's, art took a new direction under the influence of Stefan Luchian, with particularly vivid use of pigment reminiscent of folk crafts.

Contemporary painters like Lucian Grigorescu and Iorgulescu-Yor have been influenced by the French artists Cézanne and Matisse, and again use bold hues. One finds many impressionistic paintings and inexpensive prints in Bucharest's art galleries.

Little of the socialist realism school, where scenes glorifying the worker deliver a political message, is seen in the galleries. However, there is still a reluctance to try anything new or daring, for fear of appearing too Westernized.

BRANCUSI

Constantin Brancusi (1876–1957) stands out as the most impressive sculptor the country has produced. As a shepherd boy, he worked in the surrounding hills and came to know the moods of nature. Serving as an apprentice with a carpenter, he later studied at the Bucharest Academy of Fine Arts. His first nude was so realistic that it was used at the medical school in Bucharest as an anatomical model.

In the middle of the Hurez Monastery, near Tirgu Jiu, stands the church, a masterpiece of 17th century Walachian art. Inside are portraits of Constantin Brancoveanu and his family, who founded the monastery.

"The Table of Silence" is one of Brancusi's large-scale works at Tirgu Jiu, near where he grew up. Perhaps the "table" top is a millstone, and the 12 "seats" around it represent the 12 numbers on the face of a clock, suggesting that time grinds all things down.

He enrolled as a student at the Ecole des Beaux Arts in Paris and the great French sculptor, Rodin, asked him to join his studio. But Brancusi felt he wanted to break with the realism of European sculpture and preferred to support himself as a dishwasher.

He believed the nature of the artist's material determined the form of the sculpture. Since he worked with hard materials like stone, marble, steel and wood, his work had a formality to it. From his *Head of a Child*, which was somewhat like Rodin's work, he moved to more abstract works like *The Kiss*, which he would model over and over again with variations.

Brancusi was buried in Paris, but he lives on through his works displayed in museums all over the world.

FOLK ART

Through the centuries, folk art has taken many forms—from the Arges pottery decorated with bone pen and wire brush, to the peasants' homes with their quaint garden fences and entrance gates. The peasant measures his wealth in the number of hand-crafted objects and materials in his home, and a girl's dowry is made up of handmade linen and embroidery.

In demand are the Oltenian carpets, with their red and blue floral and animal designs, and the Moldavian carpets, with dark tints and a tree-of-life design. Rumanian painting on glass, of which the most famous are the glass icons of Transylvania, show striking realism and skill.

The columns of an arcade of the Palace of Mogosoaia displays delicate carving and a mosaic floor. The palace is now a museum with silver, tapestry, paintings, furniture, rare prints and other items from the 17th through the 19th centuries.

A crest of peacock feathers adorns the hat of this young man in folk costume.

Like the women of many other countries of Eastern Europe, Rumanian ladies take pride in decorating Easter eggs in bright hues and intricate patterns.

Handwoven rugs of pure wool are made on hand looms by Rumanian women working at home during the winter months.

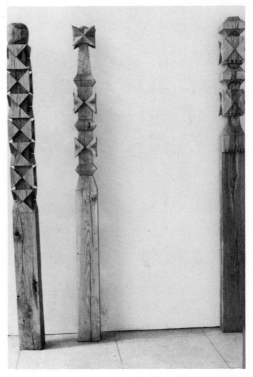

Wooden columns are carved into many shapes and patterns by the skilled hands of Rumanian craftsmen.

The bride is prepared for the ceremony at a village wedding.

This carved spoon is really a wall decoration.

Folk costumes vary from region to region, but all excel in the variety of their styles, with highly decorative embroidery worked in gold and silver thread, and trimmed with spangles and tiny beads of tinted glass.

The women wear embroidered blouses, apron skirts worn over white underskirts, and either an embroidered veil of raw silk or cap ornamented with pearls. The men wear a shirt, and trousers of coarse wool held up by a belt of cloth or leather. In winter the men embroider sheepskin vests for themselves or for sale.

LITERATURE

The earliest literature of Rumania consisted of sung poems that expressed a range of feelings from love to bravery. These ballads and tales might recall a famous battle, or express man's love of nature. Since they were not written down, each generation relied on its memory to sing the songs.

The oldest written documents were religious, written in Slavic. When the Reformation spread to Walachia and Moldavia from Western Europe, religious works began to be written in Rumanian.

In the 1800's, a group of writers of the Romantic school helped pave the way for the uniting of the states and their independence. They drew on folklore and past history to inspire the people. Among them were the poet

George Enesco, Rumania's greatest composer, conductor and musician, was a child genius, and later put Rumania on the musical map of Europe. At five he was playing the violin, and at 18 won the Paris Conservatoire's Grand Prix for violin. At 21 he formed his own chamber trio in Paris, developing friendships with Casals, Saint-Saens and Ravel. He wrote two Rumanian Rhapsodies and Suites for Orchestra, using native folk music in the works. When he died in 1955 an International Violin Competition was started in his name. Today many visit his birthplace in a town renamed for him.

Several great Rumanian literary figures all came from the Jassy region in Moldavia, and their minds were shaped in the exciting atmosphere of the state university. Since the 1800's Jassy has been an intellectual seedbed for the changes that have taken place in the country. Among the Jassy writers, Ion Creanga (1837–89), was the author of fairy tales.

he possibly originated the "dada" movement, which attacked all conventional art forms and encouraged more daring works. He wrote poems in French about the Moldavian countryside where he was born. Eugene Ionesco left when the Fascist régime was established and moved to Paris. He is best known for plays such as "Rhinoceros" and "The Bald Primadonna" that are part of the Theatre of the Absurd.

PRESS

Rumanians are hungry for the printed word and a barrage of newspapers, books and magazines pour out of the government's editorial and printing offices in Bucharest. Officials point

Mihail Eminescu and Andrei Musesianu, who proclaimed the idea of national and moral unity.

Their counterparts in this century were the writers that came to prominence between the two World Wars, some of whom are still producing today. They had a patriotic message between the wars that easily meshed with the Communist philosophy after World War II. Among them were Tudor Arghezi, Rumania's foremost modern poet, who changed from a sombre style to writing optimistic verses about peasants' revolts. He died in 1967.

At least two writers left Rumania to settle permanently in France. Tristan Tzara fled his homeland in World War I to escape conscription. In the European artistic community,

The traditions of Rumanian culture have been expressed beautifully in the poetry of Mihail Eminescu (1850–89), world-renowned poet, whose works have been translated into many languages.

At Cluj, the cultural capital of Transylvania, one sees evidences of both Rumanian and Hungarian influences. The Hungarians frequently occupied Transylvania and there is a sizable Hungarian population in the province. At the University, courses are offered in both languages, as are plays, operas, newspapers and books. In the city are Gothic churches, a link with the Catholic west, and a gleaming Orthodox cathedral, fashioned after the Byzantine style of Eastern Europe.

proudly to the many foreign literary works that are being translated, and the foreign books for sale. There are a variety of well-printed and illustrated art magazines printed in the country.

The newspapers are controlled by the government. Government officials justify censorship of foreign news stories because of the danger of upsetting international relations.

Apparently student newspapers have more leeway. Each has a letters column where sometimes radical ideas reach print. Foreign newspapers are permitted in the country, unlike many other Eastern European nations.

On the grounds of Peles Castle is the smaller Pelisor Castle—Pelisor meaning "little Peles." It is in the Renaissance style, but sits in a garden laid out along English lines. Pelisor is used as a hotel for artists and writers.

53

The Patriarchate Church, on the Hill of the Patriarchate in Bucharest, reflects the Byzantine influence. But some feel it has a uniquely Rumanian quality in its design, being less heavy than Byzantine churches of Greece or Yugoslavia. This church has kept all its towers, in spite of earthquakes and insurrections such as the uprising against the wealthy landowners in 1655. The church draws a big attendance of worshippers. The interior glows with the gold-painted icons of saints.

RELIGION

For some years after the Communists came to power religion was curtailed, even though freedom of worship is guaranteed to all citizens. Many churches were closed, church lands seized, and priests accused of subversive activities.

In the 1960's the government adopted a more tolerant attitude and spent money to restore churches and monasteries. Although this was done mainly to make them tourist attractions, it also drew some Rumanians back to a religious life. The Rumanian Church joined the World Council of Churches in 1961.

About 80 per cent of the people belong to the Rumanian Orthodox Church, an extremely active branch of the Orthodox group, with an extensive monastic network. The Greek Catholic or Uniate Church, which recognized the authority of the Pope, and to which 10 per

The buildings of the University of Bucharest, built between 1856 and 1869, line the Boulevard of the Republic, one of the main streets of the city.

cent of the people belonged, was forced by the Communists to break with the Vatican in 1948 and join the Orthodox Church.

Today Roman Catholics, largely Hungarian, make up about 9 per cent of the population; the rest are Calvinists, Jews and Lutherans.

EDUCATION

In Rumania, all schools are run by the Government, and much importance is placed on education. Many schools have been built, and teachers trained, since the Communists came to power. Their goal is for everyone in the country to be able to read and write. Today, one out of 5 Rumanians is taking some kind of schooling. A worker may take technical courses at night to improve his skills, or a farmer may study livestock breeding by a correspondence course.

After pre-school education (for 3-to-7-year olds), every child must finish 8 years of primary school. Among courses in the primary school are Rumanian, social studies, science, a foreign language, and plenty of mathematics.

After primary school the young person may go to a secondary, technical or teacher training school for up to four years. The most gifted

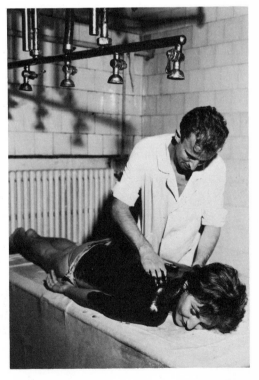

This girl is getting a cold mud-bath at Eforie Nord, a Black Sea health resort famous for its charming hotels and gardens.

Bucharest's largest sports arena, the August 23rd Stadium, seats almost 80,000 people. Nearby is a Romanesque outdoor theatre, an artificial skating rink, and a tower for parachute jumping.

young people attend a secondary school and then go to one of the country's 13 universities. All education and textbooks are free, and students living away from home may receive Government stipends or scholarships to support themselves.

Scientific research is carried on by the 10,000 workers of the Rumanian Academy in Bucharest, which has 100 separate institutes. Advances have been made in mathematics, physics, chemistry, medicine, the technical sciences, and other scientific fields.

SPORTS AND RECREATIONS

As are other Eastern Europeans, Rumanians are sports enthusiasts. Weekend athletes organize themselves into dozens of amateur sports clubs to compete in such sports as cycling,

The beach of Eforie Nord lies just south of Constanta.

The circus in Bucharest is held in a marble and glass building in a shape that suggests a circus tent.

swimming, soccer and tennis. They also have a sport, "*oina*," which is like American baseball. To contribute to "patriotic education and physical tempering," the Government sponsors mountain hikes, bike races, holiday camps, and athletic competitions for the students.

The 23rd of August Sports Centre in Bucharest has a stadium seating 80,000, with facilities for basketball, volleyball, tennis, indoor hand-ball, and indoor skating. Another sports center in Bucharest, the Dynamo, has a 400-meter-long concrete cycling track, a stadium with a racing track, and a soccer field.

Internationally, Rumania's athletes have taken firsts in hand-ball, kayak canoeing, target shooting, wrestling, gymnastics, Rugby and horse racing. Olympics in the past 20 years have brought them 11 gold medals.

In 1969 their "Cinderella" team reached the challenge round in the Davis Cup tennis competition against the United States, but was eliminated in matches at Cleveland, Ohio.

This is not the French Riviera, but the Lido Hotel in Bucharest.

The Black Sea port of Constanta, which has recently been enlarged to take care of increased cargo trade and tourists, has important shipbuilding, metal and food industries. Among Black Sea ports, Constanta is second only to the Soviet Union's Odessa in volume of shipping.

5. THE ECONOMY

As WITH THE surrounding countries, Rumania was once a rural, backward land. For centuries under Turkish rule, peasants lived off the food grown on a plot of land, and their sons divided it to make even smaller plots. In the 1800's the country painfully moved from a type of late feudalism into capitalism. Factories and mines were built with foreign investments—mostly English and French. The foreigners preferred to ship the minerals and raw materials back to their own countries and then sell the Rumanians the expensive finished products. Still, there were now some opportunities for the farmers to leave the land and get better paying jobs.

This situation existed until World War II, when all industries were taken over by the Germans. After the war, the Russians and Rumanians jointly took them over, drastically overhauling the nation's economy along Communist lines. All factories, mines, banks and

At this shop in Bucharest, the customer has a wide choice of textiles, many produced in Rumania.

transportation networks were nationalized—run by the government. Private enterprise was done away with except for small farms and craft operations. Many wealthy people suddenly found themselves without a penny because their bank accounts were seized.

Several joint Soviet-Rumanian companies were set up with names like Sovrompetrol (petroleum prospecting and processing), and Sovromtransport (shipping). These ventures gave the Soviet Union trade advantages over other countries in developing Rumania's natural resources.

In 1954 these joint companies were abolished, as Rumania rid itself of Russian influence and now operated them itself. In 1964, Rumania boldly rejected the Soviet plan for East European economic integration and insisted on the right to its own domestic and foreign policy. It did not want to be a supplier of raw materials and produce to more developed Communist nations, and thus have to depend on buying finished products back from them. Rumania still belongs to the Council for Mutual Economic Assistance (COMECON) of Eastern Europe, but is an inactive member.

Men in a motor car factory work on motor shafts.

This sprawling state farm raises pigs under the most modern conditions.

AGRICULTURE

Collective farms (also called co-operative farms) were set up in 1949 to boost farm production. Families in the collective farm pool their land and farm equipment, dividing profits from the sales among themselves. The state encourages the starting of collective farms by excusing them from paying taxes for the first few years and not setting high production quotas for the farm at the beginning. Farmers on collectives may grow produce on small private plots for their own use and to sell.

State farms, which account for only 14 per cent of the farming land, are model farms where the farmers work as employees of the state and earn a fixed salary. Besides the state and collective farms, there are a few small privately-owned farms.

Rumania's 43,000,000 acres of farm land are generally sown in summer and fall crops. Principal products grown in the plains are grains—wheat, rye, barley, oats and maize. Higher areas are good for vineyards, orchards, vegetables and industrial crops such as hemp and flax. Horned cattle, sheep, hogs and poultry are also raised in the hilly regions.

On a state farm, tobacco is tended with modern farm machinery.

FORESTRY

Each year forests in the Carpathians yield tons of timber, still another gift from the land. Taking over ownership of forests, the state has replanted them, and built roads to get the lumber out. Such care is exercised by the state to make sure there will always be a supply of wood, that a private citizen can be fined heavily for cutting a tree. Lumberjacks cut the trees with power saws in the high mountain valleys and bring them to the rivers in trucks. Then the

The Carpathian forests provide Rumania with one of its most valuable resources—timber. Conifers (seen here) account for only one-quarter of the forest area, the rest being hardwoods such as oak and beech.

logs are bound with steel cables to make rafts and the lumberjacks skilfully float them down river to mills to be sawed into boards.

INDUSTRY

Although Rumania has loosened its ties with East Europe, there is still a healthy exchange of goods within these nations. About half of Rumania's trade is with all Communist nations, half with non-Communist nations. Currently Czechoslovakia is helping build power stations in Rumania, and has joined with East Germany and Poland to build a wood pulp mill there.

Symbol of the fantastic industrial growth that has taken place in the past few years is the new steel plant at Galati that began turning out steel in 1966 and has an output of 2,500,000 tons a year. By the middle 1970's it is expected to be one of Europe's largest mills. The Rumanians refused a loan from Moscow to build the plant. Unfortunately the mill is dependent on coke and iron ore from the Soviet Union to operate, and supposedly the Russians could cut off the supply any time they wanted.

FLOODS OF 1970

The floods of early 1970 struck a hard blow to the economy, and especially the Galati mill on the Danube. They were caused by heavy rains, and a heat wave that melted snow on the mountains. Dikes built to protect the mill and factories in Galati were fairly effective, but there was much damage throughout the country. Close to 200 people were killed, many farm animals were lost, as well as homes and factories.

The damage was expected to increase Rumanian dependence on the Soviet Union, but Ceausescu's firm statements to the contrary helped silence the fear. Red China and the

The August 23rd Steel Works (in foreground) in Bucharest is one of the largest plants in the country. Beyond the plant is a broad zone of new housing.

United States led in providing flood relief. Israel flew in first with relief supplies, but the United States and the Netherlands were close behind. Western companies offered to repair or replace industrial equipment which they had furnished. The Soviet Union waited a week before sending a message offering aid.

TRADE

In spite of disagreements, Rumania and the Soviet Union still plan sizable trade with each other in the early 1970's. Russia will provide Rumania with coke, iron ore, cotton and other raw materials, machine tools and heavy equipment. Rumania will deliver sea-going and river craft, steel pipes, oil and chemical products, timber and furniture, textiles and other manufactured goods.

Overall, Rumania trades with more than 100 countries, West Germany being its principal trading partner outside the Communist bloc. Its machine building industry has grown from nothing since World War II and provides valuable exports. It also sells petroleum, manganese ore, wood products, clothing and grains abroad. Imports include iron ore and coke, motor vehicles, copper, machinery and industrial equipment.

The control of the economy by planners in Bucharest seems to have worked better in Rumania than other countries with centralized economies. The industrial growth rate was around 11 per cent a year in the last half of the 1960's, higher than any other East European Communist country. Each year there are increases in most industrial sectors, but it is interesting that these production increases often fall short of government goals, which are set unrealistically high.

In spite of economic success, the country's economists are aware that a centralized economy

Oil fields at Ploesti pour out some 13,000,000 tons of crude oil a year, second in production (in Europe) only to the Soviet Union.

can create lots of paperwork and resultant inefficiency. One member of the Ministry of Petroleum admitted that "We are making some changes in administering industry because we've expanded so much. A central office just can't handle it all. But we don't need to go beyond that because everything is working very well."

Planners are working with the American Center of International Management Studies, part of the Young Men's Christian Association, in developing a computer program of input/output analysis to make economic forecasts. This should make future planning easier.

POWER

As part of the industrialization scheme, many electric plants have been built that burn coal, oil or natural gas to make electricity. Other electric plants use falling water from rivers or lakes instead of a fuel to create electricity in hydroelectric plants. Many modern "hydro" plants have been built along rivers—one river, the Bistrita, has so many plants on its banks lit up during the night that it is nicknamed "the river of lights." The largest plant is at the Iron Gates, where the Danube breaks through the mountains near Turnu Severin, and is a co-operative project between Yugoslavia and Rumania. Each country built half the dam, one set of ship locks, and a power station with 6 turbine generators.

The Iron Gates Dam pours some 5,000,000,000 kilowatt-hours of power annually into each nation. And the reservoir formed behind the 182-foot high dam has covered over a number of rapids, thus speeding and increasing river traffic.

On the Rumanian side of the river more than 3,500 buildings were relocated. A whole island on which Turks had lived since the 15th century was flooded by the project, but not before the buildings on it were taken apart and moved to another island downstream.

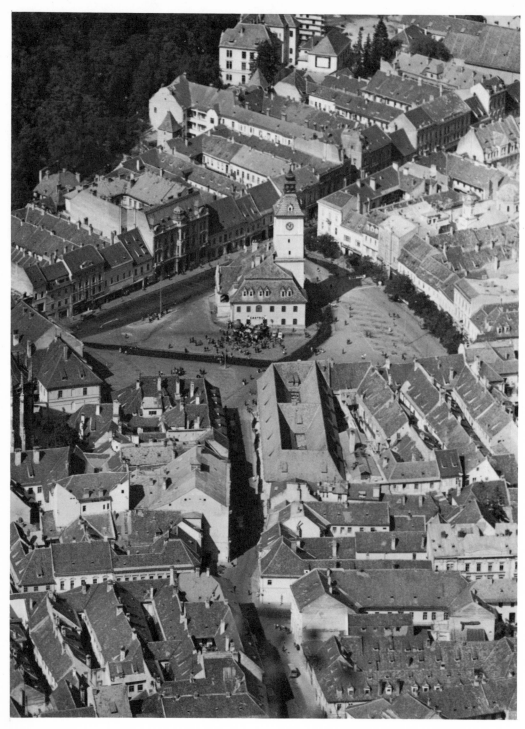

Medieval Rumania survives in this charming quarter of Brasov.